Introduction

Above & Beyond Acoustic was an idea that we talked about for years and this book and the CD and DVD held within it are proof that it finally happened. We're very happy about that. Not only because so many of you won't have been able to experience it first hand at the shows in London or LA, but also for ourselves. To be honest, it all feels a bit like a dream.

Playing live takes a huge amount of preparation and rehearsal, patience and hard work - and yet it is over in a flash. No matter how hard you try to slow down time when you are on stage, one by one the songs come and go and when you look down at the set list there are fewer and fewer moments left to savour. Before you know it, the applause dies away, the audience is heading to the bar and you're left sitting in the after-glow of a magical experience wondering "did that really happen?"

For that reason we wanted to record the experience properly, both on film and as a studio album; both versions are contained here. In addition, since this was such an important project for us, we wanted to make a commemorative special product - the book that you are holding now. It contains a selection of beautiful images from the gigs in London and LA, shot by our lovely and talented photography team: Amelia Troubridge and Fabio Affuso covered the intimate Porchester Hall shows in London and Rukes captured the exhilarating open air nights at the Greek Theatre in LA. Also included are some behind the scenes shots of the rehearsal and recording process.

We hope these images and recordings capture the spirit of those magical evenings. They give us all the opportunity to relive some of the moments that made those nights so special. At the time we thought the four dates in London would be all there was, but half way through the week we were enjoying it so much we decided we had to do more. Two sold-out shows at LA's legendary Greek Theatre have given the idea life outside London and the delicious thought that Above & Beyond Acoustic is an idea with a future. Who knows where it will end?

The bulk of the album was recorded by Bob Bradley in the spring and summer of 2013 in London and Leeds, and the live film was shot during the run of shows at London's Porchester Hall in June. Dan Sully directed the film on behalf of Vice. The album mixing and video editing was completed after the two LA shows.

The album contains all the songs we performed at the London shows in June. As well as some of the best-loved Above & Beyond and OceanLab songs from the last twelve years we included a brand new song called "Making Plans" which we'd written just before the project began. The three additional songs we performed in LA are, as yet, unrecorded, but we're all hoping there'll be an opportunity to release them in the future. "Small Moments" appears in the film but not on the album because we released it before.

We hope you enjoy our acoustic journey as much as we did. These are some of the most memorable moments we have ever experienced as Above & Beyond.

Thank you for letting us do this.

Jono, Tony and Paavo.

The Project

Above & Beyond Acoustic began life as an idea shortly after our first ever live show in Beirut in 2009. On that occasion we tried to bring our dance music productions to life for the first time, in front of 8,000 people. It was a hugely ambitious and challenging exercise and whilst it was certainly enjoyable and memorable, we all felt afterwards that attempting to play with the precision of computers (we didn't want to mime) is an ultimately thankless task. No matter how well you play, and we played pretty well, the gap between human performance and sequenced was always obvious, if not to the audience then certainly to us. It was not surprising that the next live gig we did was altogether more organic and intimate, in the basket of a hot air balloon with two acoustic guitars, a tiny piano and Zoë singing un-amplified. At 3,000 feet over the English countryside and in the windless silence only a hot air balloon can provide, it was a magical experience for us and the audience of twelve lucky enough to share it. In the basket that day was Pete Tong, whose surprise and delight at what he'd witnessed gave us great encouragement to do something similar, but more ambitious.

Our experiences in Beirut and in the balloon taught us one thing, that we needed a proper musical director if we were to do something live again, to take the stress of planning, arranging and executing away from us and leave us with the fun part - the playing.

Whilst there were many people in the frame for the job, in the end the choice was staring us in the face. Prior to joining Above & Beyond, Tony had been in a band with a guitarist and producer called Bob Bradley, and the two had kept in touch, musically and socially, ever since. Bob had made small but important contributions to Above & Beyond's music over the years, when his unique musical vision overlapped with what we were trying to do. His first job had been a chill-out mix of "Far From In Love" in 2002, on which it's possible to hear many of the hallmarks of the Acoustic band he would make real twelve years later: the trip hop beats, the lush strings, even the James Bond/Twin Peaks guitar. Bob has honed his art in the intervening years and as well as building a hugely successful TV and film music business has found time to add occasional beats, vibes and inspiration to our three studio albums.

We had an initial meeting with Bob in our studios and outlined what we wanted to do - essentially MTV Unplugged, but with style and wit. We asked him to work up one song as a demo and after a few weeks he sent a prototype of "Love Is Not Enough". It appears on the album much as it sounded then: simply incredible. We agreed a time frame and started a collaborative process that took six months and resulted in new arrangements of twelve of our best loved songs, the basis of a live show and the demos for an album.

The process involved heading up to Leeds from time to time, to write and record our individual parts in Bob's studio. This was the first time we'd been 'produced' as a band and we all found it a hugely enjoyable experience; being encouraged, coached and cajoled to express yourself on your favourite instrument with someone else worrying about how it all fits together for a change - it's very liberating.

Part of our shared vision for the album and show was to incorporate live strings. We've always used strings on our albums but Bob encouraged us to think even bigger than we would normally in this regard. He introduced us to Chris Egan who writes string arrangements for film and TV out of Abbey Road studios. It was a wonderful day out of our normal studio experience to go to this landmark venue and talk with Chris about how the strings would sound. His working method was refreshingly old-school: despite having an office full of samples and sequencing software, he works the arrangements out in his head and writes them down on paper with a pencil. He doesn't do demos: the first time anyone else hears Chris' string arrangements is when they are played by the orchestra for the first time.

And so it was in March when we went to Angel Studios to hear our 24 piece string orchestra record their parts. All string players sight-read, so there are no rehearsals as such. There would be a brief discussion, Chris would wave his baton and, instantly, the orchestra would play perfect string instrumentals of the songs we knew so well. Seeing orchestral sheet music with "Alone Tonight" or "On A Good Day" written on the top was thrilling in itself. To hear it brought to life by some of the best players in the land - that was mind-blowing.

The Shows

We've definitely played in some memorable places over the years, beaches in Brazil, clubs from Ibiza to India, even deep in the Mojave Desert. Yet few have produced the feelings that we experienced on the four nights at Porchester Hall in June.

Our search for the right venue had taken us right across London. We saw lots of suitable places but all were missing that special something: until we found ourselves in Bayswater's Porchester Hall. Everyone instantly fell in love with the old place: the chandeliers, the decor, the wooden carved panels, the long musical history - it was perfect.

Our director, Dan Sully, elected to go with a classical, timeless look for the shows and the film, with a simple colour palette that was sympathetic to the antique interior of Porchester Hall and the acoustic nature of the music. It was our brilliant lighting designer, Neil Marsh, who decided to use the huge old 1960 Hollywood lamps "Mole Richardson Skypans", (conveniently just re-issued for the first time). Neil wanted to keep the 1960's feel and so there were no new bulbs, just old fashioned tungsten spots, a big fairy light festoon and Porchester Hall's original chandeliers wired into the lighting desk. Add a few uplighters to illuminate the coving and the look was complete, 1960's chic to complement a band playing instruments from the '60's - and wearing clothes to match.

So much of what we were doing in these shows was new to us as

Above & Beyond. Of course we were playing the instruments that we have known all our lives, but playing our greatest hits with a full band set-up to some of our most dedicated fans made it all brand new.

We were certainly far from our comfort zone: instead of the usual light shows and huge speakers it was just us, our songs, our wooden instruments and this amazing new acoustic band. When you're in a dark club it's a bit anonymous at times - you could be anywhere in the world. But when we were on stage at Porchester Hall we couldn't have been anywhere other than in that space and at that time. Every show was different, every minute unique and special.

One of the things that is so enjoyable about playing live is when you look across the line at your fellow musicians and share the moment. It could be a smile, a nod or even just a glance, but it is wonderful. You can hear the entire song being performed, the swell of the strings, the pluck of the harp, the bass, the drums, the singing - and you are just

a small but important part of it. It's almost like you are part of the audience and the band at the same time.

It was evident on stage just how close we had become as a band. We had spent weeks rehearsing and had come to love and respect our new musical family to the point where we had complete confidence in them all. In a live situation you can never expect everything to go without a hitch and you need to be prepared for that - we're only human, after all. But the amazing thing was that, somehow, it really was alright on the night - pretty much every night. Zoë was so sick that week, she was getting out of bed and getting in a cab to come to the venue just in time for the shows. But she's such a professional you would never have known it - when she started singing the room melted.

I think our new vocalists Annie and Alex had the hardest jobs, standing in for singers that had become so well loved, but they both gained a lot of new fans over the week. And so it was for

the rest of the band. It felt like we had been playing together for years.

And then there was the audience.

We knew from emails and tweets that some of our most loyal and ardent fans were going to be at the shows and we also knew they had no idea what they were letting themselves in for. The intimate nature of the gigs meant they had to sit quietly for most of the show instead of the customary dancing about we usually encourage. And we were certainly taking liberties with the songs, with new arrangements, surprising instrumentation, new singers and even new lyrics to contend with. We knew we were asking a lot.

As it turned out, the reaction in the room on all four nights in London, and later in LA, was nothing short of incredible. We saw it, every night, on faces only a few feet away from us. After all that hard work and all that concentration, when the music would start dying away and people would start cheering - it gives us goosebumps just thinking about it.

The Songs

There were lots of reasons why we wanted to do Above & Beyond Acoustic, but essentially it was a showcase for our songs. We've always had this belief that good songs can connect with people, musically and melodically, in a way that goes far beyond instrumental music. There's a magic when you put words and music together that is hard to explain and the longer we're together, the more gigs we do and the more albums we put out, the more we realise just how important that really is.

In most cases, before we start thinking about dance production, we write songs - mostly on piano or over a simple backing track. Only when we have the song working do we go to the next stage - so hearing them naked is very natural to us. But given how much we owe to the ongoing thirst for electronic music around the world, we couldn't help wondering if we were removing everything that makes Above & Beyond relevant in 2013. Would our songs hold up as compelling pieces of music in an 'unplugged' context? Could they still

connect with our fans in the same way? The one thing we did know was that, at the end of a DJ set, the acoustic mixes of "On A Good Day" and "Satellite" that we already had were proving to be wonderful sing-along moments. But would that hold true for over an hour?

We couldn't know the answer to any of these questions, so it took a certain amount of belief and bloodymindedness to take that leap of faith.

One of the things we've always done is use our own experiences and feelings when writing songs. There's nothing new in this, it's what most bands do, but it does seem to be rare in dance music for some reason. The exact details of the source of the songs, the relationships, the personal triumphs and failures, aren't critical: we just feel that songs written honestly are more powerful.

Given the way we write, it is often the case that we write more 'song' than we need. This was the case with "Sun & Moon" where the second verse was chopped completely from the club mix but resurrected for these Acoustic shows. But this wasn't always so: when we wrote "Alone Tonight" ten years ago it was as a dance track and so we had to reverse engineer a second verse in order to make it work in a traditional form. This gave us an interesting challenge, since the story has effectively been public knowledge for a decade, and any new lyrics would be being heard first in a live situation. In the end we wrote the second verse in the present day, looking back, almost as a piece of musical theatre for Alex to perform on the night. The songs were transformed in other ways, too. Bob had suggested splicing

"Satellite" and "Stealing Time" together for musical reasons - they're both in the same key - but lyrically they were a perfect match. "Satellite" was written about the long distance phase of Paavo's relationship with his now wife, when Sachi was in Japan and Paavo was in London and "Stealing Time" is an essay about life in Above & Beyond - so the two work perfectly as a duet.

For all these reasons we were really looking forward to performing these songs live. It's one thing to turn down the volume during "Sun & Moon" and hear the audience at one of our DJ gigs singing along, but to live through twelve songs, line by line, word for word, with an audience five feet in front of you - that's another thing entirely.

We hoped that the honesty that we always strive for in our songs would lend itself to a performance in such an intimate space. But there is an added layer of honesty in live performance that gives the stories a realism and personality that comes from a story being told first hand.

It was on that basis that Tony agreed to sing "Making Plans". We usually

outsource the singing of the songs after we write them and indeed Alex Vargas has come up trumps on a brilliant recording of "Making Plans" for our next album, but in amongst all the orchestration and clever arrangements we wanted to give people a glimpse into our songwriting process at its rawest and perform one song just as a trio. In the event, our string arranger Chris Egan loved the song so much he asked if he could arrange strings for it for free, and how could we refuse?

We deliberately didn't announce the songs before we did them - the arrangements are mostly so different we wanted to add a layer of surprise to proceedings - and those moments of realisation were always very enjoyable, for us and the audience. As the songs progressed it was wonderful to watch the reactions of the audience close hand as the stories played out; there were people holding hands, hugging, mouthing the words with eyes closed, some crying, many singing out loud. It was humbling to experience the living connection people have with this material - as songwriters this is exactly what you set out to achieve.

Miracle

Don't they know
That there's something going on?
What they're harming
With their indecision?
And who will be left
Standing when I'm gone?
There'll be nothing left but a vision

And it's too easy to
Turn a blind eye to the light
It's too easy to bow
Your head and pray
But there are some times
When you should try
To find your voice
And this is one voice
That you must find today

Are you hoping for a miracle
As the ice caps melt away?
No use hoping for a miracle
There's a price we'll have to pay

Don't they know that there's
Something they can do?
To be sure of tomorrow's tomorrow
And too late is too late for me and you
No more time left for you to borrow

And it's too easy to
Turn a blind eye to the light
It's too easy to bow

Your head and pray
But there are some times
When you should try
To find your voice
And this is one voice
That you must find today

Are you hoping for a miracle
As the ice caps melt away?
No use hoping for a miracle
There's a price we'll have to pay
Are you hoping for a miracle?
Are you hoping for a miracle?

You Got To Go

Dream on little dreamer
This is how it all begins
Dream on little dreamer
This is how it all begins

Move your feet
Feel how sweet it is
Dream on little dreamer
Follow all of your signs

You got to gather up what you need
You got to choose a direction
And when the moment
Is right for you, you got to go
You got to keep your ideals high
You got to know that the sky
Belongs to no one
And you know you got to go

Dream on little dreamer
This is how it all begins
Keep on little dreamer
Keep hold of all that you are

Move your feet
Feel how sweet it is
Dream on little dreamer
Follow all of your signs

You got to gather up what you need
You got to choose a direction
And when the moment
Is right for you, you got to go
You got to keep your ideals high
You got to know that the sky
Belongs to no one
And you know you got to go
You got to go, you got to go

You got to gather up what you need
You got to choose a direction
And when the moment
Is right for you, you got to go
You got to keep your ideals high
You got to know that the sky
Belongs to no one
And you know you got to go
You got to go, you got to go
Dream on little dreamer
Follow all of your own signs
You got to go, you got to go

Satellite / Stealing Time

My love is like footsteps in the snow
Baby
I follow you everywhere you go
Baby
The palest light has come to wake you
But you will never realise
That I inspire the dreams that guide you
Baby

I follow the winds that bring the cold
Baby
I'll light a fire in your soul
Baby
The lightest touch of feathers falling
My love may be invisible
But I inspire the dreams that guide you
Baby

You're a half a world away
But in my mind I whisper
Every single word you say
And before you sleep at night
You pray to me, your lucky star
Your singing satellite
Your satellite, your singing satellite
Your satellite
You're half a world away

I'm stealing time from my own life
All the hours that god sends
I'm flying high on my red-eye
And winding down the window

My future is a Valentine
Stolen in the perfect crime
And I know I'm living out of line
But with a blazing smile I'll die

You're a half a world away
But in my mind I whisper
Every single word you say
And before you sleep at night
You pray to me, your lucky star
Your singing satellite

Thing Called Love

There was a time there was a place
But there was fear inside
A witty line to save my face
A parachute of pride

To cross the line takes a tiny step
But will the spark cause
The bridge to burn?
My fear entwined with my regret
I beat a path for safe return

There's a thing called love
That we all forget
And it's a wasted love
That we all regret
You live your life just once
So don't forget about
A thing called love
Don't forget, forget about
A thing called love

So here we are, we're just the same
And you will never know
My secret plan
How close we came
To share another road

And have I lost my only chance
To tell you how I feel inside?
Is it just me I'd like to know
Or are we all just a little blind?

There's a thing called love
That we all forget
And it's a wasted love
That we all regret
You live your life just once
So don't forget about
A thing called love
Don't forget, forget about
A thing called love

Can't Sleep

4:30 am, I'm awake again
Singing to the dark
Through open eyes
While dreaming I see
Only you and me
Stuck between desire
And compromise

If I said I want you back I'd be a liar
There's nothing left
Of us to long for any more

But inside the ashes
Burns an endless fire
And every night
I can't help reaching out for more

And I can't sleep
You're so far away from me
And I can't sleep, and I can't sleep
And I can't sleep
You're so far away from me
And I can't sleep, and I can't sleep

You're leaving these scars
Scattered round my heart
A road map of the places
You have been
But I can't escape
Can't wash this away
When love has burned
Your mark so deep within

If I said I want you back I'd be a liar
There's nothing left
Of us to long for any more
But inside the ashes
Burns an endless fire
And every night
I can't help reaching out for more

And I can't sleep
You're so far away from me
And I can't sleep, and I can't sleep

Sun & Moon

It's raining, it's pouring
A black sky is falling
It's cold tonight
You gave me your answer - goodbye
Now I'm all on my own tonight

But when the big wheel starts to spin
You can never know the odds
If you don't play you'll never win
We were in heaven, you and I
When I lay with you
And closed my eyes
Our fingers touched the sky

I'm sorry baby
You were the sun and moon to me
I'll never get over you
You'll never get over me

You held back and lost out
You gave in to each doubt
And walked away
A final embrace
You won't turn, I won't chase
Nothing more to say

But when the big wheel starts to spin
You can never know the odds
If you don't play you'll never win
We were in heaven, you and I
When I lay with you
And closed my eyes

Our fingers touched the sky

I'm sorry baby
You were the sun and moon to me
I'll never get over you
You'll never get over me

Good For Me

To be with you is easy
I know you're good for me
This feeling inside me
Oh it sends me sky high

To be with you is easy
I know you're good for me
This feeling inside me
Oh it sends me sky high

You're good for me, my baby
So good for me, my love
You're good for me, my baby
So good for me, oh love

To feel for you is easy - oh baby
I know you're good for me
This feeling inside me
Oh it sends me sky high

You're good for me, my baby
So good for me, my love
You're good for me, my baby
So good for me, oh love

You're good for me, my baby
So good for me, my love
You're good for me, my baby
So good for me, oh love

Sirens Of The Sea

I cannot resist your call
I cannot resist your call

Take my hand, take my hand
Yeah, take my hand
Follow me, follow me, yeah, let's go
To the sand, to the sand, the purest sand
Into the sea, into the sea, yeah, let's go

Out beyond the water's edge
Far out past the coral ledge
Underneath the diamond dancing lights
Chase the world from far below
Silent sleeping indigo
Drifting out into the endless night

I cannot resist your call
I cannot resist your call

Take my hand, take my hand
Yeah, take my hand
Follow me, follow me, yeah, let's go
To the sand, to the sand, the purest sand
Into the sea, into the sea, yeah, let's go

Leaving reason far behind
Nothing here is cruel or kind

Only your desire to set me free
Let us lie here, all alone
Worn away like river stone
Let us be the sirens of the sea

I cannot resist your call

Love Is Not Enough

Well, I've had too many a
Good cry for you
Well, this is my time to say
Goodbye to you

In my heart of hearts
I know there's more love left for you
But love is not enough, I've learned
To see the journey through

This is not yours alone
It hurts me too
Please don't say you don't care
I know you do

In my heart of hearts
I know there's more love left for you
But love is not enough, I've learned
To see the journey through

Love is not enough for me
If it screams when you hold it
Love is not enough for me
Love is hurting if it screams
Oh, if it's screaming out loud

I've been screaming for love
Love is not enough

In my heart of hearts
I know there's more love left for you
But love is not enough, I've learned
To see the journey through

On A Good Day

A little bit lost and a little bit lonely
A little bit cold here, a little bit of fear

But I hold on and I feel strong
And I know that I can
I'm getting used to it
Lit the fuse to it
Like to know who I am

Been talking to myself forever, yeah
And how I wish I knew me better, yeah
Still sitting on a shelf but never
Never seen the sun shine brighter
And it feels like me on a good day

I'm a little bit hemmed in
A little bit isolated
A little bit hopeful
A little bit calm

But I hold on and I feel strong
And I know that I can
I'm getting used to it
Lit the fuse to it

Like to know who I am

Been talking to myself forever, yeah
And how I wish I knew me better, yeah
Still sitting on a shelf but never
Never seen the sun shine brighter
And it feels like me on a good day

Alone Tonight

Slipping sideways, silver stars collide
And fade away
Just like our love that died
And there is nowhere
In this universe to hide
From you tonight

I've wrestled with angels all my life
It's always the haloes and the wings
That keep you blind
And if I had fought with all
The strength I held inside
I wouldn't be out here
Alone tonight
I wouldn't be standing
Alone tonight

Alone tonight
Just like the western star
I'm sinking
The angels curse me blind with
Straight and crooked thinking

I've been crossing out the words

I left unsaid
From the epilogue
Left lying in my head
Where there is poetry
And tragedy unread
Until tonight

There's no other angel
Quite like you
They broke the mould
A thousand pieces icy blue
And though I tried
To realign them - like I do
You went your own way
And I did too
So here I am

Alone tonight
Just like the western star
I'm sinking
The angels curse me blind with
Straight and crooked thinking

Making Plans

Time held its breath
A motionless spell of rapture
Across the room
A memory had been captured
And through the years
Though distance lay between us
I carried your torch
To illuminate the darkness

And I still lose myself
In that orange glowing moment
When your upturned face
Seemed to answer all my questions
But when I ask myself
As I do from time to time now
Where it all went wrong
Is there really any point
In making plans?
In making plans?

So I made my vows
In the last slow hours of morning
As I lay you down
I heard you whisper me a warning

But then we lost ourselves
In that orange glowing moment
When your upturned face
Seemed to answer all my questions
But when I ask myself
As I do from time to time now
Where it all went wrong
Is there really any point
In making plans?
In making plans?

And I still lose myself
I still lose myself
Making plans

All songs written by Above & Beyond (Jono Grant, Tony McGuinness, Paavo Siljamäki). Except Miracle, Satellite, Sirens Of The Sea, On A Good Day written by Above & Beyond and Justine Suissa. You Got To Go, Good For Me written by Above & Beyond and Zoë Johnston. Love Is Not Enough written by Above & Beyond, Andrew Bayer and Zoë Johnston. Can't Sleep written by Above & Beyond and Ashley Tomberlin. Sun & Moon written by Above & Beyond, Justine Suissa, and Sorcha Shepherd.

All tracks published by Involved Publishing Ltd. Except Miracle, Sirens Of The Sea and On A Good Day published by Involved Publishing Ltd/ Copyright Control. Satellite and Good For Me published by Warner/Chappell Music Holland/Copyright Control. Stealing Time and Alone Tonight published by Warner/Chappell Music Holland. Can't Sleep published by Warner/Chappell Music Holland/

Involved Publishing Ltd. Sun & Moon published by Involved Publishing Ltd/Copyright Control.

Above & Beyond Acoustic (Studio Album) produced, arranged and recorded by Bob Bradley. Additional production and arrangement by Above & Beyond. Mixed by Andy Bradfield for 365 Artists at Studio A, London, except Love Is Not Enough mixed by Bob Bradley. Mastered by Miles Showell at Abbey Road.

Recorded at Chadwick Lodge, Leeds. Vocals on Miracle, Satellite, Can't Sleep, Sirens Of The Sea, On A Good Day by Annie Drury. Vocals on You Got To Go, Good For Me, Love Is Not Enough by Zoë Johnston. Vocals on Stealing Time, Thing Called Love, Sun & Moon, Alone Tonight by Alex Vargas. Vocals on Making Plans by Tony McGuinness. Electric and Acoustic Guitar, Mandolin and Ukulele by Bob Bradley and Tony McGuinness. Piano by Paavo Siljamäki. Rhodes by

Jono Grant. Electric Bass by Bob Bradley. Double Bass by Neil Harland. Live drums by Shawn Lee and Bob Bradley. Brass by Tim Hutton. Mellotron, Dulcitone, Vibraphone and Glockenspiel by Bob Bradley. Backing vocals by Annie Drury, Zoë Johnson, Alex Vargas and Bob Bradley. Programming by Bob Bradley. Engineered by Nick McEnally.

Orchestra recorded at Angel Studios. String arrangements by Chris Egan and Bob Bradley except Making Plans arranged by Chris Egan. Strings produced by Jez Murphy. Score supervisor Trystan Francis. Contractor Dom Kelly. Assistant contractor James Marangone. Violins by Jackie Shave, Warren Zielinski, Magnus Johnston, Natalia Bonner, Tom Gould, Nina Foster, Gillon Cameron, Eva Þórarinsdóttir, Kerenza Peacock, Marije Ploemacher, Jim Dickenson, Gareth Griffiths, Sam Wickramasinghe and Alice Hall. Violas by Bruce White, Melanie Martin, Cheryl Law and Felix Tanner. Cellos by Caroline

Dale, Chris Worsey, Victoria Simonsen and Clare Hinton. Double Bass by The Callipygian Mary Scully and Rich Pryce. Harp by Skaila Kanga.

Above & Beyond Acoustic (Live Performance at Porchester Hall, London) Musical Director - Bob Bradley. Assistant Musical Director - Sebastian "Bid" Beresford. Arranged by Bob Bradley and Above & Beyond (Jono Grant, Tony McGuinness, Paavo Siljamäki). Mixed by Bob Bradley and Above & Beyond.

Recorded live at Porchester Hall, London. Vocals on Miracle, Satellite, Can't Sleep, Sirens Of The Sea, On A Good Day by Annie Drury. Vocals on You Got To Go, Good For Me, Love Is Not Enough by Zoë Johnston. Vocals on Stealing Time, Thing Called Love, Sun & Moon, Alone Tonight by Alex Vargas. Vocals on Making Plans by Tony McGuinness. Backing vocals by Annie Drury, Zoë Johnston and Alex

Vargas. Piano, Dulcitone, Vibraphone and Cello by Paavo Siljamäki. Fender Rhodes and Vibraphone by Jono Grant. Vocals, Fender Jazzmaster, Acoustic Guitar, Vibraphone and Mandolin by Tony McGuinness. Acoustic Guitar and Sweeping Brush by Bob Bradley. Trumpet, Trombone, Mellotron, Acoustic Guitar and Glockenspiel by Tim Hutton. Electric and Double Bass by Neil Harland. Drums and Percussion by Sebastian "Bid" Beresford. Additional Drums and Percussion by Joelle Barker. Additional Vibraphone by Donald Ross Skinner. String quartet - Dirty Pretty Strings (Amy Langley - Cello, Amy Stanford - Viola, Gita Harcourt - Violin, Rosie Langley - Violin). Harp by Siobhan Swider. Production Manager - Mark Townson. Production Crew - Stage Miracles. Staging - All Access Staging and Productions Ltd. Lighting - Colour Sound Experiment. Grand Piano Tuner - Joe Dodd. Lighting Director - Neil Marsh. Front of House Sound - Graham "Hutch" Hutchinson. Monitor Audio -

Tom Howat. Guitar and Back Line Tech - Donald Ross Skinner. Tour Manager - Seamus Morley. Tour Manager's assistant - Kata Farkas.

Above & Beyond Acoustic Live at Porchester Hall Film. Directed by Dan Sully. Produced by VICE and Above & Beyond. Full Live & Film Production credits included within DVD. Art Direction and Imagery by Big Active. Band photos by Amelia Troubridge, Fabio Affuso and Barbara Doux. Additional Photography by Paavo Siljamäki and Zach Cordner. Mediabook production by Rowleys: London. Above & Beyond Management by James Grant, Steve Heaver, Giuliana Hilton and Leena Lewis. Anjunabeats Label Management by Allan McGrath and Michael Farrell. Above & Beyond Bookings by Paul Morris and Matt Rodriguez at AM Only (World excluding Europe), Alex Hardee and Tom Schroeder at Coda (Europe). UK Press by Matt Learmouth at Alchemy PR.

Musicians

Working on Above & Beyond Acoustic was a completely different experience for the three of us. Bob's role changed things instantly - we became a band working with a producer, not the producers per se. This in itself was incredibly liberating: holding a guitar is a lot less stressful than holding the reins.

Once rehearsals got going we were also working in a much bigger band set-up than we were used to, surrounded by many talented and inspiring musicians, all with their own unique personalities. Being one of fifteen is also a very different experience than being solo or one of two. Your world shrinks a bit, it's more cosy and safe. But when you start to play together and add your own small part to the whole, big, lush sound that the fifteen-piece band could make, you feel part of something so much bigger. In some ways, it is like you've co-opted the instruments, the sounds, the abilities even, of everyone else in the room and it is an incredible feeling.

The design of the band came from Bob: as the album started to take shape he always had one eye on the future band line up. We knew his musical pallette included only the coolest instrumentation, classic references and ideas that have stood the test of time: shades of Portishead, DJ Shadow and John Barry to name but three. Bob used his vision and contacts to bring in some excellent additions to the Above & Beyond set-up, shaping the band to fit the sound we all wanted. Our aim was always to get the best players we could. Finding new voices to sing our most iconic and well-loved songs was no mean feat but Bob set about the task unfazed – as did the vocalists we eventually found. Bob's first suggestion was Alex Vargas from Denmark. Alex has everything we look for in a vocalist, a beautiful, emotional voice capable of covering a wide range: he can be smooth and sultry, but also full-on and anthemic.

Joining us for the OceanLab songs was the enchanting Annie Drury. Bob was tipped off about her as a special talent and tracked her down to a bar in Yorkshire where she was singing and playing piano. She stole the show there, as she did in Above & Beyond. Annie has a really beautiful English voice that has that special ability to be both gorgeously delicate and incredibly strong at the same time.

And then there was Zoë Johnston. We wanted to work with Zoë ever since we heard Faithless' "Crazy English Summer" – a beautiful, timeless song of love and doubt that could grace any A&B album. It's both a joy and an honour to be able to work so closely with Zoë now, and the fact that she battled

illness and throat issues in London to perform in the style that she did speaks volumes about her talent. We introduced Zoë as being from Mars - there is no one on Earth as good as her.

Our drummer and assistant MD Sebastian Beresford, aka Bid, was a shoe-in for us, having anchored our Beirut electronic live show. Bid's CV includes Edwin Starr, Rodrigues and Leftfield and his enthusiasm matches his experience. The drummer is always the heartbeat of any band and in Bid we couldn't have wished for a stronger, healthier one. He was joined by good friend Joelle Barker who played additional drums and percussion. They've known each other for years and played together like hand in glove.

In amongst so much talent, our secret weapon was multi-instrumentalist Tim Hutton. He's played with Groove Armada, The Prodigy and Ian Brown before, so we knew we were getting a class act, but his musical versatility simply knocked us for six: there doesn't seem to be an instrument he can't play. On the nights themselves he played all the brass parts, vibraphone, guitar, glockenspiel and keyboards.

Then there was Neil Harmond, the bass player. We wanted someone who was as good a double bass player as they were an electric bass player, which is quite hard to find, but Neil is brilliant at both and added the perfect blend of feel and flair to all the tracks.

Our string section for the Porchester Hall shows was a quartet called Dirty Pretty Strings, who had worked with Paloma Faith and Ed Harcourt previously. Joined by Siobahn Swider - our brilliant harpist - our classical section looked the part and played it even better, oozing elegance in everything they did.

The LA shows had much the same line-up, but we were joined on stage for one song by Sonny Moore, aka Skrillex. He'd enjoyed the first show so much we invited him to play some guitar on the Sunday night, a moment that delighted audience and band alike. His presence was testament to the gorgeous spontaneity of live performance.

Like any band, when we played together on stage we became something far greater than the sum of our parts. We were Group Therapy in action.

Thank Yous

Above & Beyond would like to thank Adam Sellers, Al Judd, Alex Hardee, Alex Hoffman, Alex Vargas, Alice Hall, all at All Access Staging & Productions Ltd, Allan McGrath, Amelia Troubridge, Amy Wickman, Andrew Bayer, Andrew Bonwick, Andy Bradfield, Annie Drury, Avril & Malcolm Grant, Barbara Doux, Ben Barfoot, Bob Bradley, Bree Horn, Bruce White, Caroline Dale, Charlotte & Finn Morley, Cheryl Law, Chris Egan, Chris Worsey, Clare Hinton, Corentin Kerisit, Dan Sully, Daphne Chen, David Waxman, Dirty Pretty Strings (Amy Langley, Amy Stanford, Gita Harcourt, Rosie Langley), Dom Donnelly, Dom Kelly, Donald Ross Skinner, Dylan Ryan Byrne, Eddie, Andrew, Rob & all at Ministry Of Sound, Eddie Ruxton, Edina Gabri, Eunice Park, Eva Þórarinsdóttir, Fabio Affuso, Felix Tanner, Gareth Griffiths, Gareth Jones, Gillon Cameron, Giselle Grant, Giuliana Hilton, Graham Hutchinson, Greg Eggebeen, Helen Zheng, Ian Gibson, Jackie Shave, James Grant, James Marangone, Jez Murphy, Jim Dickenson, Joe Dodd, Joe Heaver, Joelle Barker, Josh Neuman, Justin Webb, Kam Sandhu, Kata Farkas, Kenton Mitchell, Kerenza Peacock, Laura Bruneau, Leena Lewis, Liam, Liz, Rachel, Sarah & Ben McGuinness, Lisa Liu, Lohan Presencer, Lucy Blair, Magnus Johnston, Marc Mancus, Marije Ploemacher, Mark Ellis-Cope, Mark Townson, Mary Scully, Mat, Markus, Phil & all at Big Active, Matt Learmouth, Maya Gordon, Melanie Martin, Michael Farrell, Michael Johnson, Miles Showell, Mimi Flemming, Mollie Runacus, Myles Desenberg, Natalia Bonner, Neil Harland, Neil Marsh, Neil Ribbens, Nick Feldman, Nick McEnally, Nigel Pollard, Nina Foster, all at Red-TX, Patrick Moxey, Rich Pryce, Richard Marshall, Ron Pac, Rusnè Daugèlaitè, RY X, Ryan Boey, Sachiko, Aino, Taiyo, Aapo, Riitta, Meeri & Lauri Siljamäki, Sam Alpert, Sam Campbell, Sam Wickramasinghe, Seamus Morley, Sebastian Beresford, Shawn Lee, Silvija Stanisic, Simon Allard, Simon Barrington, Siobhan Swider, Skaila Kanga, Sonny Moore, all at Stage Miracles, Steve Heaver, Steve Satterthwaite & all at Red Light Management, SuzAnn Brantner, Theo Gupta, Tim Hutton, Toby Raiden, Tom Gould, Tom Howat, Tom Schroeder, Tommas Arnby, Trystan Francis, Victoria Simonsen, Warren Zielinski, Will Hicks, Zoë Johnston, Zofia Plonczak.

Thank you to everyone who shared the very special shows at Porchester Hall and the Greek Theatre with us.